Access

THE POWER OF
PRAISE AND
WORSHIP

Jason Nelson

Contents

Foreword

Now after six days Jesus took Peter, James, and John his brother, led them up on a high mountain by themselves; and He was transfigured before them. His face shone like the sun, and His clothes became as white as the light. And behold, Moses and Elijah appeared to them, talking with Him. Then Peter answered and said to Jesus, "Lord, it is good for us to be here; if You wish, let us make here three tabernacles: one for You, one for Moses, and one for Elijah." While he was still speaking, behold, a bright cloud overshadowed them; and suddenly a voice came out of the cloud, saying, "This is My beloved Son, in whom I am well pleased. Hear Him!" And when the disciples heard it, they fell on their faces and were greatly afraid. But Jesus came and touched them and said, "Arise, and do not be afraid." When they had lifted up their eyes, they saw no one but Jesus only." Matthew 17:1-8 NKJV

Ascending precedes access. The principle revealed in this pronounced scriptural moment offers us peculiar keys to understanding the grace afforded to those who would journey with God to an elevated posture of heart and spirit. The Mount of Transfiguration is not just a revelational narrative; it is a relational objective. It was the favored opportunity to see "naked" God. Glory unclothed. What a remarkable privilege of sight and substance given to the inner 3; for it marked the first time that Christ took off His "Jesus clothes" and gave them a view of what humanity had been shrouding. One of the first intimations we gain is that not everyone will be afforded the opportunity to "go up". It is not because of God playing "favorites". Indeed, however, it has to do with proximity based upon purpose and assignment. The more weighty the task given, the closer we must be to Him. The more urgent the call, the more committed to the answer we must be. As John the Revelator on the Isle of Patmos, we must "come up hither" to be shown the "hereafter" which must be.

Another perspective still, those who are called to go up gain the favored view of another "economy" at work. There is a realm that "eyes have not seen, ears have not heard, neither has it entered into the hearts of men..." that offers us a peering into the DONE things of God. It is a visual that mandates we transcend beyond the locality of our familiarity and engage, with wonder and awe, an invisible reality; not seen by the obvious telling of the eye.

As this moment turns, we see another gem of understanding glimmering in the dark. Ascension requires maturity. It is in our reflexive nature to feel the need to "eisegete" a revelational experience with our own perspective & context. Peter's impetuous reaction to the moment "Let us build three tabernacles" exposed him as one who really did not understand the privilege of his presence in this God moment. He didn't understand that he did not possess the capacity to "interpret" this phenomenon that he had never seen. He was talking from HIS sense of "sense" not understanding that his input was not needed. He did not know that this was a place to be THERE, be AWARE, but be QUIET. What we must learn is that access into certain places does not require our input. Our presence there is our only participation required. And it is in being there that all things will be revealed to us. There will be moments that will only need our attendance and attention; not our agenda. "Hear Him."

Finally, we see one more lasting nugget of revelation that cannot be ignored. At each point of worship, we are offered an opportunity to ascend; to come up into a revelation of something we've never experienced before. It requires that we change our posture to see ourselves in the light of His presence. When you offer proximity and access to those who profess relationship with you, yet they maintain their distance, that is a prime indication of 2 significant things: 1) They fear unworthiness to be in your presence or 2) there is something already occupying that space and to enter into true covenant with you means they have remove, or at best reorder, something in their lives; disrupting comfort or certitude. Both of these ideas hinder the freely-given access granted to us. Our fears and facts are barriers to taking advantage of the grace of entering into precious moments with Him who calls us higher. We must allow Christ to deal with the "religions" so engrained in our souls that have the potential to exclude us from the benefits of His presence. Any process, system, relationship that manipulated our fears or facts as threats to realizing eternal purpose in His presence must be broken away from. Every unordained, self-obligatory relationship must be ended so that we can begin to live in and out the MAXIMUM CAPACITY of God's grace & glory. "Arise and do not be afraid" is allowance of a change of disposition that allows us to "lift up our heads" to see the open heaven above and the divine possibilities within. We, like Peter, James and John, are being CALLED UP to GO INTO. Through the vehicle of worship, we have been given upward access to realize that Christ alone is not only worthy to be answered; but worthy only to be adored.

"When they had lifted up their eyes, they saw no one but Jesus only."

Access Granted.

Bishop L. Spenser Smith

Introduction

Sound fills churches week after week, permeating the atmosphere: a hymn, a popular radio hit, even an instrumental song. Voices in the choir join with the instruments as hearts become full and tears flow. Parishioners lift their hands, engaging in corporate praise and worship. This happens almost automatically as most regular church attendees fall in line with a desire to experience the Presence of the Lord.

Some worship with a sense of obligation as that is their understanding of how every service starts. They think, "I might as well join in", even if their hearts aren't in it. In their minds, services begins with an obligatory offering of songs meant to engage the audience. Others feel the urge to join in as their favorite song is rendered by the praise and worship team.

Some sit and watch hoping it will all be over soon. They aren't at church for the worship. They're attending based on tradition. There are also those who tolerate worship but really prefer to just hear the preached Word.

Then, there are those who show up with a heart to engage in worship seeking to have an intimate encounter with God.

As you can see, there are several reasons people participate in worship and not all are actively engaged. This culture is pervasive in many churches, and the disinterest in worship most likely stems from a lack of understanding the power of it. When a person understands the strength that worshippers wield, they willingly engage in the act of worship with a steadfast desire to see the glory of the Lord in a tangible way.

We cannot allow our pursuit of God to be defiled. In some cases, the idea of worship has become sacrosanct and the object of our worship, God, has become secondary. The Lord has always been the object of our worship. Throughout the history of worship, the concept of worship and the purpose of worship have been at odds. The concept of worship covers the human and divine interaction while the purpose has always been relationship between God and His creation, mankind. Humanity has a penchant for lifting the concept of worship above the purpose of worship. This is evident in the interaction of Cain and Abel when they bring offerings to The Lord in Genesis 4. Cain worshipped via the concept thus his offering was not relational in nature. It was conceptual. Cain operated from the perspective that any offering would suffice as long as an offering was given. Abel, conversely, offered to The Lord precisely what he knew would be acceptable. There was a level of care and concern that Abel exemplified that was absent in the worship that Cain offered. God had no respect or regard for Cain and his offering but had respect for Abel and his offering.

God took the opportunity to teach a very valuable lesson regarding worship. While He accepted Abel and his offering he told Cain that he had missed the point of this interaction. God instructed Cain that if he had done well, his offering would have been accepted. But if he didn't do well that sin was crouched at the door waiting to exercise its desire on Cain. God also told Cain that he didn't have to give in to the desire of sin but that he should master and control it. The parallels are clear that one who properly engages in worship from God's perspective should also possess the ability to master sin. This gives credence to Jude 24. Now unto Him that is able to keep you from falling and to present you faultless before the presence of his glory. When we spend time in worship building relationship, Jesus, in turn, provides us with the ability to not fall prey to sin and its desires. We must focus our attention on The Lord and seek to please Him in our worship. We must abandon concepts of worship that end in frivolity and personal satisfaction choosing instead to dig deeper in the purpose of worship which is to build a greater relationship with The Lord.

I hope to spark in every reader of this book a desire to experience, through worship, the presence of the Lord daily. These daily encounters will augment the gathering together of all the saints in a crescendo of unified hearts and minds. **Access** will unlock simple keys to how worship reshapes ideologies, reignites passion and restore worship to the forefront of every lover of God. **Access** will take you through 7 doors that will bring clarity and understanding about the power and importance of worship and praise.

The fear (reverence) of the Lord is the beginning of wisdom and the knowledge of the holy is understanding. (Proverbs 9:10 NIV)

Reverence in the act of worship is an expression of deep respect tinged with awe. Simply put, worship is a mechanism that releases wisdom. Worship has the ability to unlock the treasures of Heaven and you can gain knowledge of the holy, which reveals knowledge of who the reverence is directed toward. It has the power to release wisdom and understanding and it is a key to living a life of grace, power, and effectiveness. While others are sitting on the sidelines, you can engage in worship and watch it open doors to spheres of understanding, enlightenment and deeper relationship that you've never imagined.

What follows are 7 chapters that are represented as doors. Each door will give insight into what worship is, our roles in worship and the expected responses when we choose to Access those doors. As you enter each door, I believe you'll see a breakdown of walls that have been obstacles to life changing praise and worship to The Lord.

Door 1

Instruction Is Key and Obedience Is Access

C hange is inevitable, and shifting is unavoidable. Jennie B. Wilson, a gospel songwriter, has said, "Time is filled of swift transition. Naught of earth unmoved can stand." We serve a God who is on the move (Genesis 1:2). We move from strength to strength (Psalms 84:7), grow from faith to faith (Romans 1:17), and are changed from glory to glory (2 Corinthians 3:18). We are most certainly on the move as we follow the presence of God, thus we must also be ready to move and shift with Him.

A manifestation of glory is attached to the move of God. It was so in the days of Moses with the pillar of cloud by day and the pillar of fire by night (Exodus 13:21). It was so in the days of Joshua with the movement of the Ark of the Testimony (Joshua 3). It was so in the days of David with the Ark as well (2 Samuel 6). When God decides to move and transition us, He gives us an instruction. Our obedience to the instructions of the Lord is an act of worship. It means we are submitting ourselves to His will and plan for our lives. Often submitting to God's will

11

means being able to heed instructions even if your present life has to be uprooted for obedience to occur. That level of obedience leads to a path of deeper relationship and intense worship. The Bible gives us clear insight into this function of obedience as worship. What follows is a quick study of the man through whom worship is initially released. In Genesis 11, we are introduced to a man named Abram and a brief understanding of his genealogy.

Terah, the father of Abram, intended to travel to Canaan but stopped in a place called Haran. Haran became a substitute destination and, as a result, all of the family of Terah established a home in the wrong place. After Terah, whose name means station or delay, settled in the wrong place, The Lord altered the life of Abram.

In Genesis 12, God spoke to Abram and instructed him to leave his country, his kindred and his father's house. Abram followed the instruction knowing that God had given a promise to bless him and make him a blessing. The promise also declared that all the families of the earth would be blessed through Abram. What Abram didn't understand at the time was that Abraham would be released out of him only if the instructions were followed.

Access

Abram's willingness to hear and follow the instructions became the catalyst for all of mankind to partake in the blessing of Abraham through adoption by Jesus Christ. Abram's obedience was not just about leaving his homeland. The instructions weren't just about leaving his homeland. The instructions were to leave country, kindred and his father's house. Those three elements (country, kindred, father's house) housed limitations that had to be broken through obedience.

The country represented the place of comfort for Abram. It was where he matured, where he found and married his wife, Sarai, and where he built his wealth. The country also represented the place where success could be found. Abram had planted seed in that land and received harvest. His current success was all tied to the land where he lived. The land of Haran had proven to be profitable to Abram. Sometimes the instructions of The Lord don't make total sense because being obedient will force us to move into places of discomfort and the unknown. But Abram was willing to abandon his current land for a land of promise.

The part of the instruction regarding leaving his kindred can be difficult because kindred represents people who one has grown up with. You know them. They know you.

Departing from them can be a major challenge. Obedience will often call for us to leave those who are only comfortable with the iteration of what currently exists. Too often, we remain in places too long to assuage the fears, doubts, and mindsets of people who cannot see beyond their perceptions of us, where we should be, or how we should live. They still see us as "knee high to a jack rabbit" or the younger version of ourselves. They cannot imagine that what God has instructed us to do, in order for us to transition to a new place, could be aptly applied to us. These people might constantly remind us of who we used to be and rehearse the past as if the best of our lives are behind us. Kindred can be the greatest enemy to real growth because the trappings of comfort are with them.

The concept of a father's house really refers to the methodology of a parent. Terah's house represented a failure to arrive at a place of destiny because of the past. It dealt with the traditions that one holds dear that might not mesh with instructions received. It's extremely dangerous to filter the instructions of the Lord through a traditional mindset that is based on the past generation's understanding of movement and progress. The instruction to Abram was all encompassing to ensure that real progress was made when obedience occurred.

Our fathers' generations might interpret progress as going from a tube television to a flat screen even though 4K televisions exist. Tradition makes big moves seem impossible, improbable, or deleterious to who you must become. Leaving a father's house means making a decision to break tradition and allow God to set new parameters for our lives.

In Genesis 17, Abram's name was changed to Abraham and he subsequently sired Isaac, the promise, with Sarah, formerly Sarai. Abraham was challenged a few years later to follow instructions again in Genesis 22. God instructed Abraham to sacrifice his beloved son, Isaac, in a place that He would show him. Abraham was instinctively obedient and rose early the next morning, chopped the wood and prepared Isaac and two servants for the journey to, what he learns will be, Mount Moriah. Three days later, Abraham, Isaac, and the servants arrived at the base of the mountain. The discourse here set the stage for an amazing scenario from which we can learn.

Abraham told the servants to stay with the donkeys while he and Isaac went up the mountain to worship and return. This is the first mention of the word worship in the Bible.

The instruction from the Lord was to sacrifice. The word worship was not mentioned by the Lord. Abraham understood that his obedience to the Lord was an act of worship. Worship here in the text means to bow or sink down and prostrate oneself to God, who is superior to us. Obedience to the Word of the Lord means submitting to His will and understanding that His will and plan is greater than anything we could ever imagine on our own.

God doesn't always give us reasons for His plans, but we know they are always good. Romans 8:28 says, "All things work together for good to them that love God and are called according to His purpose." Also, note that worship here isn't about a song, tempo, melody or tune. It is about a life bowed down in worship to God. If we only pursue worship in the course of verses and choruses, we are missing out on the real benefit of engagement with the presence of the Lord. He desires a full relationship with each of us. We must be upright in our pursuit of Him. There are times when we don't always seek God or desire to follow His instructions when it means losing things that we love. Often, we are tested to ensure that what we have isn't more important to us than our relationship with God. This is the kind of test that Abraham was subjected to when God spoke to him to sacrifice Isaac.

God told Abraham to sacrifice Isaac. Abraham declared that they would worship and return. Sacrifice meant to kill, cut up, and burn an offering. There is no question about that at all. God instructed Abraham to kill his promised son (the promise He gave Abraham). Abraham has spent far too much time in relationship with God, so he instinctively knows God's voice. He obeyed.

Worship would culminate in sacrificing Isaac. Thus, we understand that worship—real worship—requires sacrifice. Something must be given to God for worship to take place. The altar must have something placed on it. Romans 12:1 informs us that we are the sacrifice in worship. "I beg you brothers, by the mercies of God, that you present your bodies a living sacrifice, holy, acceptable unto God." This is our reasonable act of worship.

Again, worship is a life bowed down in humble submission to God's will. The altar is meant to consume anything not like God. Anything that doesn't belong in your destiny and anything that does not work for the purpose that God has spoken will be burned up by the fire when we put ourselves on the altar. This act of worship opens doors and gives access to the believer that was meant for us but not accessible until you are obedient because instruction is a key and obedience is access.

Abraham went up the mountain knowing that God desired two elements: blood and death. Both elements would play an important role when God formally introduced worship to Israel at Passover and the Day of Atonement. A lamb would be killed and its blood would be spread on the door posts and lintels. This sign would ensure that death would pass over the house that was "covered" by the blood. Obedience was imperative in this case, as disobedience would lead to death of the first born male in that house. The eyes of death looked for blood and the promise of God would protect that house from the terror of that night. Every house in Egypt that did not have the token of blood suffered loss of every living first-born male in one night. This final plague to Egypt sealed the exodus for the Children of Israel as the Pharaoh finally relented and let God's people go. This concept originated at Mount Moriah with Abraham and Isaac. Neither men knew the significance of the moment: that obedience was the access into the miraculous.

Isaac, who had clearly been briefed on what worship was, asked, "Where is the sacrifice? I see wood and I see fire but I don't see the most important part of worship: the sacrifice." Genesis 22:7-8 Abraham's response gives us another revelation on worship. If we take on the posture of worship, God will provide. A provision is significant because God provided Himself a sacrifice, thus, we know our worship is not an empty gesture. Our worship is an act of faith. We know we don't have enough to adequately give God the worship He deserves. We give what we have anyway, believing that He will provide whatever is missing.

Worship does not necessarily include singing, liturgical dancing, music of any kind nor any other modern mechanism for giving honor to the Lord. We have, unfortunately, relegated worship to the sound of music and distanced ourselves from the concept of heart, obedience to instruction, and death with fire. Romans 12:1 takes us back to the introduction of worship with its description of worship. No song, dance, mime, or praise team can be the substitute for an altar and a sacrifice. Obey the instructions and completely surrender to God's will.

Abraham built an altar and tied up Isaac. As he prepared to deliver the killing blow to Isaac, an angel appeared and told Abraham to let his son live. The angel also told Abraham that he has proven that he wouldn't hold

anything back in worship. Here is where we understand
God's description of worship: John 4 says, "The hour is
coming and now is when they that worship will do so in
spirit and in truth. With His spirit and wholly transparent.
Withholding nothing." Giving everything and placing it on
the altar is a sign that we would rather live a life of
obedience to the Lord than give an offering that will never
be an appropriate substitution. If our lives lack
obedience, we cannot be trusted with the responsibility
and privilege of crossing the threshold into the place
where we can see the glory of God manifested.

Abraham's act of obedience released provision in the
form of a ram with his horns caught in a bush to be
sacrificed in the place of Isaac. Obedience is not about
loss. It's about establishing the fact that we can be
trusted with the deep things of God. Deep calls to deep
and the obedient answer the call.

Door 2

I Am A Door

Heaven has always housed worship. There are hosts of heavenly beings whose purpose is to worship and praise the Lord. Lucifer, at one point, was the chief worshipper and a doorway that the heavenly host, as they looked at him, could see the presence of God.

Abraham, in his obedience to the instruction and worship, created a space for Jehovah-Jireh to be revealed in the earth realm. He became a door.

In Mark 10, blind Bartimaeus utilized the ability to create a door for manifestation to occur in his life. He heard the tumult of the crowd passing and inquired as to what the gathering was about. When he heard that Jesus Christ was passing by, he began to cry out with a loud voice to ensure that he was heard. When Jesus heard the cry of Bartimaeus, he stopped moving to respond. The sound of, "Son of David, have mercy on me," (Mark 10:47) was significant enough to make room for a miracle.

Bartimaeus was not afraid to annoy those who were close to him. He understood that his need was unlike theirs. He needed to be healed and regain his sight.

They were merely following Jesus to see Him work miracles. The sound of his cry opened the door for Bartimeaus to be healed. His sound built a door. We all have the ability not only to create a door, but to become a door.

Psalm 24 was written as a celebration of the entrance of the Ark of the Covenant to the City of David. The Ark of the Covenant was a symbol of the presence of the Lord. When the Ark was brought into the city, it was cause for a great celebration throughout all of Israel. King David understood the value of the presence of the Lord and made sure that He would be honored. Psalm 24 described the location where the Ark would be housed as the "hill of the Lord." David writes about who would ascend and stand in the hill. Clean hands and a pure heart were necessary components for qualifying to go up the hill of the Lord. There was an understanding that not just anybody or any mode of living was acceptable. A special standard had to be upheld in order to be considered for participation.

The ceremonial requirements aside, there were also requirements for personal sanctification. Pride was unacceptable. Proper language was required. One could not be lifted up or swear deceitfully. Honesty has always been a requirement for worship. That's why we must worship in spirit and in truth. David had insight into these requisite standards and shared them with those who were chosen to participate in the returning glory of the Lord. David incorporated these instructions in the psalm to ensure that all would remember the gravity of the assignment.

This psalm also shows us David's preparation in paving the way for ushering glory into a house. There were two different choirs set up to release the songs and sounds that would accompany the moving of the glory of the Lord. One choir was with the ark as it departed from Obededom's house. The other choir waited anxiously in the hill of the Lord to hear the sound of the approaching glory sung by those accompanying the Ark. "Who is the King of glory? The Lord strong and mighty," they sang in praise (Psalms 24:8). That particular stanza of the song was sung as the group approached the base of the hill. The choir in the hill would respond to the choir surrounding the ark. This is one of the instances in the Psalms where there was call and response. Lift up your heads was a signal to raise the gates to allow the entrance of the Ark and those who carried it on their shoulders. The gates were physical but the psalm indicates that people were also called doors. We must understand that when we properly position ourselves, we become the conduits for the glory of the Lord to be revealed and released in the earth.

As we discussed earlier, Heaven perpetually houses the sound of worship. Angels never cease to worship the Lord. Lucifer was called "the anointed cherub that covers (Ezekiel 28:14)." He was perfect in creation. His assignment was to create a sound that announced the presence of God. Whenever the sound of Lucifer was heard, Heaven knew a manifestation of the presence of God and His glory was imminent. Lucifer was beautiful: His body was made of pipes and horns and embedded with every kind of precious stone. His every movement made a sound that gave glory to the Lord God. His design was strategic in that the majestic splendor of God's glory would reflect off of Lucifer's person. Everywhere Lucifer went, he was a grand announcement of glory, majesty and the splendor of the Lord. This was a great responsibility.

Lucifer allowed the gravity of the assignment to lead him away from his purpose. He began to see himself as the origin of the Light of glory and decided to take God's throne for himself. He declared that he would exalt his throne above God's throne. He stopped singing and sounding in worship and began to merchandize himself to the other angels. The Lord immediately sensed the wicked desire of Lucifer, as he transformed from a worshipper to a merchandiser (Ezekiel 28:16). He sold his perspective and the Bible says that a third of the host of angels fell with Lucifer because he was a great salesman. Pride is a major component in the fall of Lucifer. In truth, a proud worship leader is an oxymoron. The two cannot intersect and function simultaneously.

Lucifer is the first to be fired because of a lack of performance. He had the privilege of releasing the sound of worship as an announcement of the coming of the presence of the Lord. That worship was the sound that heaven heard on a continuous basis until Lucifer decided that his position in heaven was insufficient. Pride began to seep in and worship stopped being a necessity to Lucifer. Obedience to his assignment, honoring The Lord and the privilege to have this position were seemingly forgotten for a higher personal position in Heaven. Whenever selfishness trumps the desire for God, pride is in control and things are not going to end well.

Practical applications are also abundant here. Lucifer lost his job and was evicted from Heaven because of a change in operation. He continued to use his mouth, but now started advertising instead of worshiping and singing. He began to market himself instead of glorifying the Lord. Any worship leader who spends more time defending themselves or speaking well of their own accomplishments than blessing God is in danger of becoming just like Lucifer.

A worship leader whose focus is on themselves refuses the opportunity to be a door to the glory of the Lord. Lucifer was a conduit. The light of Glory that shined on and through him did not originate in him. It was the Light of Glory that came from the One who was being announced. Lucifer was a reflector as well. When the hosts of heavenly beings saw Lucifer, a reflection of the creator was always seen.

We must allow the Lord Jesus to be seen in us. We are living epistles read of men (2 Corinthians 3:2). When others see us, they "should" see some reflection of our Savior. We are the advance sighting of the Lord on Earth, a door to His presence. We are also a gateway to deeper relationship with Jesus Christ. Refusing to live up to that responsibility puts us on the same level as Lucifer. The Lord has said that He will not share His glory with any other creature or creation. (Isaiah 42:8; 48:11) There is a penalty for usurping the glory preserved for the Lord alone. Lucifer was evicted from heaven and fell like lightning into the earth according to the testimony of Jesus Christ in Luke 10:18. He fell as an anointed cherub who covered and landed as an accuser of the brethren, satan.

We literally deserve to be fired from our positions as worshippers when we allow pride and self grandiloquent behavior to cloud our doorway and cause Christ to be hidden. There is no inherent power in being talented. Gifts and calling are without repentance (Romans 11:29). However, there is no breaking of yokes, no lifting of burdens, no one is set free or delivered, and the church is unchanged because the Lord is not present in the presentation of worship. There must be an added ingredient called the anointing of the Lord.

Many of us have stopped being anointed and have regressed into being just gifted, and the audience missed the metamorphosis because the gifting is very convincing. Isaiah 10:27 reveals that the yoke is destroyed because of the anointing. The presence of the Lord is the catalyst for yoke breaking, life changing, gratitude inducing responses here on Earth. Gifts can be awe-inspiring but gifts alone cause no change. The anointing is what drove the demons away from King Saul as David would play his harp. God will not anoint anyone whose desire is to be more important than Him. This is not to say that we shouldn't have a positive self image. We just cannot allow ourselves to become more important than God. Romans 12:3 says we shouldn't think of ourselves more highly than we ought to. That gives us justification to have positive self-worth but maintain sobriety in that regard.

Unfortunately, a luciferian complex is ubiquitous in the current climate of church culture. We have succumbed to hiring professional worship leaders whose agenda isn't promoting God but rather promoting their next event or upcoming CD. While there's nothing wrong inherently with marketing music, leading worship isn't synonymous with peddling CDs or music to the church. The main intention must remain being a doorway to the Lord.

The fall of Lucifer gives us insight as to why satan hates worshipers. Anyone who really worships God fills the role left vacant by a disobedient, proud Lucifer. Take Job whose lifestyle of worship made him a target for the enemy. Don't be overly consumed by that thought though. Remember that Job also had a hedge around him. Worshipers live a protected lifestyle and even when things happen, God always restores worshipers to a greater position. Even when it's not popular, maintain a lifestyle of worship. There is a reward for seeking God. We are doors and must operate as such in the earth (Hebrews 11:6). The unbeliever must see God and we are often the first reflection of Him that they will encounter.

Door 3

Deliberation vs Robotic Response

The intellect must be part of the worship experience.

We must understand that worship is an emotional external expression of a cerebral experience. We must think in order to become doors. If there is no thought, our expression becomes sounding brass and tinkling cymbals, and we are using muscle memory and not faith in a new glorious experience.

Psalms 47:7 instructs us to sing praises to the Lord with understanding, which in Hebrew is "sakal." Sakal means to wisely understand, to have comprehension, to have insight, or to ponder. Thinking is a component of worship and praise to God. How can we appropriately open a door to the presence of the Lord when we don't have an appropriate understanding of the object of our worship? Our comprehension of the Lord increases when we spend time with Him in prayer, commit to fasting, read the Word and consecrate ourselves. The necessity for understanding puts a demand on the worshiper to diligently seek the Lord. Understanding removes surface recognition and colloquial knowledge as satisfactory regarding worship. In the church, we have become so accustomed to using idiomatic phraseology in the context of corporate worship that we have denied the corporate experience of deep, life-changing encounters with God. A lack of understanding limits the impact the worshiper experience, creates a limit of open doors, and minimizes our ability to be conduits for the glory of the Lord.

Hosea 6 tells us that we will know as we follow on to know. We discover more of The Lord as we walk with Him. There are realms of revelation that are unlocked as we seek to understand Him in a greater way. If we don't pursue Him daily, we defraud ourselves of available insight into who our Lord is. A lack of understanding gives way to impersonal worship and praise that has no real changing effect. We often release an automated praise that lacks real sincerity because it is based on instructions from a person we perceive as a cheerleader instead of a worship leader. We must relinquish the ideology that says I will only respond when I'm instructed to do so. This process creates a vacuum in the worship experience where few are transformed and God is not welcomed by us due to inauthentic offerings. We must think, consider, perceive, and understand before we engage in meaningful praise and worship.

Our main objective is to create space for the Glory of the Lord to be revealed. We are created for His glory. Even every one that is called by My Name: I have created him for My Glory, I have formed him (Isaiah 43:7). Revelations 4:11 says, "Thou art worthy, O Lord, to receive glory and honor and power: for thou hast created all things, and for they pleasure they are and were created." This has always been the intent of God. Our responsibility is to discern and discover ways to become and remain conduits for glory to be revealed and released. Proverbs says, "Wisdom is the principle thing." Get wisdom, and gain an understanding.

The concept of thought included in praise and worship can be found in 2 Chronicles 20. Jehoshaphat was instructed by a prophetic word that the battle he faced was not his but the Lord's. Jehoshaphat made the decision to respond to the word of the Lord by thinking about what was declared and how he and Judah should respond. He broke the tradition of war by sending the praisers and worshipers ahead of the fighting army. The instruction was to sing a song that considered the goodness of God declaring that His mercy was everlasting. Thus, praise was the appropriate response to goodness and mercy. The fact that all the people took time to consider the goodness of the Lord and respond in kind created an accelerated action from God. The Lord set up an ambush against the enemies of Judah and destroyed them before Judah even arrived at the scene of the battle. (I will discuss this further in later chapters.)

God is great and greatly to be praised. Psalm 145:3 indicates that the psalmist took time to consider who God is and what the appropriate response should be. The level of praise should match the understanding of the greatness of God. If we take the time to consider, understand, perceive, and think about God before we engaged in praise and worship, we would remove the robotics and rote responses from our worship experience. The culture that we would create in the corporate worship experience would redefine how we perceive those moments. We would be able to experience the manifest presence of God in new and exciting ways. Moses' "show me your glory" experience would be our own. The glory of The Lord would fill the space and we would be changed in His presence. Healing and deliverance would happen spontaneously in the atmosphere. The door would open and all would be impacted substantially. We must think and open doors to the presence of The Lord for our benefit and the benefit of others.

Door 4

Corporate Worship

Worship can be facilitated in conversational agreement. Isaiah 6 details the conversation between two cherubim declaring the holiness of God and the breadth of His glory covering the whole earth. We must never dismiss the power of corporate worship. The agreement of the majesty of Jesus Christ creates a space of glory and presence in the midst of the worshipers. Where two or three are gathered in the Name of Jesus Christ, He is there in the midst of them. (Matthew 18:20)

O magnify The Lord with me and let us exalt His name together. (Psalms 34:3)

Something happens when believers unite toward the common goal of releasing and revealing the presence of the Lord. Unity pulls on the presence of the Lord like little else. The day of Pentecost revealed the grace attached to a unified pursuit and mindset. In that moment, they were all in one place with one accord, and the movement of God released the Holy Spirit that sat on each of them like tongues of fire. That kind of manifestation is found when hearts are linked in the spirit and the goal is the presence of the Lord Jesus Christ. Unified pursuit is a construct of praise and worship that releases power and manifestation for the believer.

In 2 Chronicles 5, we find details of the completion of the Tabernacle of Solomon. The Ark of the Testimony is situated in His place and the staves are arranged to indicate that the presence of the Lord had found a permanent resting place. The presence of the Lord was so great that the Levites chose to leave their normal regimen and joined in with the minstrels and singers in the choir. This is a great indicator to us that we must often abandon our liturgy for the sake of the glory of the Lord. There are times when our rituals and programs become a barrier to the presence of God manifesting in our midst. We must be willing to allow the Lord to have His way even if what we have planned must be discarded. Sometimes the preacher must become the worship leader or vice versa. There will be times when singers must declare the word of the Lord to the house instead of releasing melodic expression. At other times, the planned set list must be amended for the sake of an encounter that will shift the dynamic of the house forever.

Access

The Bible indicates that singers and musicians in worship had one voice. The unity was so strong that multiple people sounded as a single individual, and the results were astounding (2 Chronicles 5:13). The presence of the Lord descended in a cloud and filled the tabernacle. The "kabod" or weighty nature of the Lord was so profound that the priests pressed to the floor and could not stand in the presence of the Lord. Here we find another truth. Worship has the ability to pull on the power and presence of God until no human song or articulation is sufficient. God Himself releases a strength, healing, and deliverance that no song can produce alone. There are times when we must stand back and allow the Lord to work as only He can. We often defeat the purpose of our pursuit of God because we invite the Lord to show up and then posture ourselves as if we know more than the Almighty. He is omnipotent and we must acknowledge His sovereignty even when He decides He will minister Himself. We must tell the Lord, "Have your way."

Unity in corporate worship also releases victory in the lives of believers. Again, 2 Chronicles 20 illustrates this by giving us a glimpse into the life of Jehoshaphat when Judah is on the verge of being attacked by the armies of Moab, Ammon, and Mount Seir. The people and the King

of Judah utilized two tools that every believer is armed
with: prayer and praise. Jehoshaphat prayed to the Lord,
asking for assistance, acknowledging that they don't
know what else to do. The Lord sent word that this battle
was His to fight and that the people should position
themselves on the cliff of Ziz to see the salvation of the
Lord. Jehoshaphat decided to do the unthinkable when
going to battle by putting the soldiers behind the singers
and musicians. He sent praise before the fighters
believing The Lord would do just what he said. The King
of Judah established a unified chorus that would become
the battle cry for victory: "Praise The Lord for His mercy
endures forever." When they began to sing this chorus of
victory, the Lord moved before they arrived and cause
confusion to set in on the enemy. The armies destroyed
one another and the fight was over when Judah arrived
on the scene.

Unified, corporate worship is a weapon against the
enemy. This is why satan fights against unity in sacred
arts and music departments consistently. A unified front
in worship sends the whole house into the safety of the
presence of the Lord. It's not colloquial to say,
"Magnify The Lord with me and let us exalt His Name
together." It's an admonition that unity should be a part
of every worship experience. Having a solidarity of mind,

intent, pursuit, and heart is essential whenever worshipping the Lord is on the agenda. Notice that God's arithmetic adds power exponentially when unity is present. The sound of one is powerful but adding the chorus of like-minded believers changes the power quotient and makes victory and deliverance that much easier to achieve. We must understand that agreement creates space for the miraculous power of the Lord to be unveiled in amazing ways. "Where two agree as touching, whatever they ask will be done by our Father who is in heaven will do it for you." (Matthew 18:19).

Corporate worship is agreement on a mass scale and that performance should happen in the midst of a gathering of the people of God. We must lay aside our personal agendas, idiosyncrasies, biases, and mindsets for the sake of unity. We must learn to find a place of agreement in the corporate setting to release a glory that we have not seen.

In 1 Samuel 10, we can see that a corporate gathering of the prophets sets an atmosphere for others to prophesy. Saul was so immersed in the culture established by the band of prophets that he was changed into another man as he began to prophesy though he wasn't a prophet. Those who witnessed the phenomenon wondered if Saul

Access

was among the prophets. This moment didn't give Saul a new function or title. It merely opened a window into the realm of the prophetic that Saul was able to operate as if he were a prophet.

The presence of a gathering of prophets was enough to trigger a response in someone outside of that space. "Oh magnify The Lord with me and let us exalt His name together" (Psalms 34:3) is an admonition that the gathering of worshippers has the ability to open up heaven over all of those who desire to participate.

That is the blessing of being around like-minded people regarding worship. The corporate setting allows those who are disconnected to join in the cloud of witnesses and engage the presence of the Lord with the group. It's a healing mechanism when those who are being assailed by the enemy can be consoled by the presence of the Lord in corporate worship. Never allow those who are weak to be left in the cold. Invite them into the corporate setting with love, showing them the benefit of a corporate response. Lift up praise and worship together and activate the blessings attached to a heavenly response.

Door 5

Modeled From Heaven

Matthew 6:9-10 After this manner pray: Our Father which is in heaven, hallowed be thy Name. Thy kingdom come, Thy will be done in earth as it is in heaven.

This prayer is the model by which each of us should live and pray. Heaven has established the truth of God's desire for worship. Worship should happen according to the way God's desire is established already in heaven. We must adopt the same methodology to elicit the appropriate response that heaven receives. The precedent has already been set in heaven and that image is what we must present.

The image of worship for the Children of Israel was based on the design the Lord originated in Heaven with Lucifer. The challenge of the worship leader is very complex for this reason. The leader must usher the congregants into the presence of God with a level of competence that goes beyond that of a rank amateur. Several elements that go into properly leading the people into an encounter with God. There is the understanding that the leader is taking the people on a journey that he or she has already undertaken. It is understood that the doors to His Presence for that day have already been discovered. It is expected that the song selection has been crafted with the mindset that victory and breakthrough are the result. The worship leader must get a feel for the audience and, in real time, make adjustments that propel the people into a personal pursuit that was initiated by the worship team. Also, the worship leader has to be sensitive enough to recognize that self has no place in the context of worship. The fact that the leader may be greatly gifted has no impact on the pursuit of God's presence. God gave the gift, and He is not impressed by its use. The heart is always the key to pleasing God and experiencing His presence. Leading with our gifts will only tickle the ears of the flesh and fail to move the heart of God or the other worshippers. They must be led in a heart journey to the face of God.

The danger of leading with your gift is found in the chronicles of the former Angel of the Lord named Lucifer. Isaiah 14 and Ezekiel 28 both give insight into who Lucifer was. The eviction of Lucifer from heaven didn't stop worship from continuously being released in heaven. That eviction did, however, create a vacancy that man has the ability to now fill. We are created to worship and glorify God. We have the privilege of worshipping the Lord but we must not forget that worship isn't a human construct. It's a divine construct in which we are graced to participate. The Lord delineated His ideal for worship in Exodus when He gave the instructions to Moses to create the Tabernacle, utensils, the garments and, most importantly, the Ark of the covenant which would be the direct corresponding element that represents the presence of The Lord. These instructions laid out a comprehensive plan and blueprint that had to be followed with great care. The plans for the implements of the tabernacle were as pertinent as the personnel who would work in the tabernacle and serve the Lord and the people. The Lord chose Aaron to be the mediation for all of Israel and would worship one for all. He became the representative for an entire nation.

Aaron served as the High Priest for the Children of Israel. The zenith of his responsibilities was to enter into the Holy of Holies on the Day of Atonement, pour blood on the Mercy Seat, and experience the Glory of The Lord on behalf of the whole nation. The days that led up to the day of Atonement were all about preparing for the Glory of God. For seven days, Aaron had to separate and consecrate himself for the sake of everyone else. It was imperative that he be ready when the time came to go into the Holy of Holies. Failure to prepare would cost him his life. Aaron had to offer a sacrifice and take the blood from the lamb and place it on his right earlobe, right thumb, and right big toe. He had to wear the blood for seven days. The dried blood would be a constant reminder that something had to die in order for the Glory of God to be revealed on the Day of Atonement. This was an indicator that God has a preset expectation of what worship looks like and what it smells like.

Aaron also had to wear the proper garments in order to get into the presence of The Lord. God had given very clear instructions on the construction of the garments that Aaron would wear and instructions for the generations that followed. The garments were designed to fit Aaron and could not be altered once completed. This indicates that the worshipper must fit the garment. God will not alter His expectation for us. We must fit His expectation. Many times we offer God something that doesn't fit into His desires and we become belligerent when He doesn't respond to our liking. He is God. He accepts what He chooses to accept. Our preference for worship must take a back seat to His desire and mandate for proper and acceptable worship. Some praise-and-worship teams fail to create an atmosphere for God's presence because the worship that was offered didn't fit into God's blueprint for worship. For God to be pleased, we must follow instructions without any deviation and accept what is offered.

The strength of worship is found in the integrity of the worshipper to give God what He desires. Failure to oblige God costs us the precious encounters that enable us to fend off the enemy and share the Love and Grace of God with others. For Aaron, it meant certain death (Exodus 28:35). Aaron was careful to fulfill all the requirements because a nation needed worship to happen. Upon entering the Holy of Holies, Aaron would feel his way to the Mercy Seat by faith. The truth of the matter is the Holy of Holies was the darkest place in the worship experience for Aaron. The closer he got to the presence of God housed in the Ark of the Covenant, the less Aaron's eyes were needed.

Worship leaders should not be afraid of the dark places that God calls them into. God dwells in the dark places of the Tabernacle. Faith is a major requirement in the worship experience. Aaron had to have confidence in his obedience to the instructions and faith that God would meet him on behalf of the people. For us, faith is needed to successfully navigate the holy places God has called us to lead others into.

Worship leaders must also have a mature level of understanding when navigating the presence of The Lord, and they must take the people where we have already been. This means that it is imperative for the worship leader to maintain a consistent personal lifestyle of praise and worship. It is extremely difficult to lead a congregation into a place one has never been. The Holy of Holies is not a place for novices. In the days of Moses, a novice was not allowed in the most holy place. There was a requirement that the Levites train from the age of 25 and begin serving at the age of 30.

God also instituted a rule that a worship leader must be adept in the Torah. In the same manner, the modern day leader should have a competent grasp of the Holy Writ. How can we accurately describe God to the people if we don't have a grasp of His Word? Knowing scripture also aids in building a language between songs that encourages the congregation to remain engaged in the worship experience. In the context of worship, very few things are worse than a worship leader who tries to lead with their gift but has nothing of merit to say to the people. We should not allow ourselves to be gifted and empty. We, as well other believers, deserve better than that, and so does the Lord. We must "study to show ourselves approved and a workman who doesn't need to be ashamed rightly dividing the Word of Truth." (2 Timothy 2:15).

We walk by faith and not by sight. The worship and praise that we give to God is given based on His desire, and faith must be a part of our offering to our Heavenly Father. Hebrews 11 shows us that we must believe that God does exist and He created everything that exists, and that He is a rewarder of those who diligently seek Him. The chase is what God desires from us. We must seek Him in every season of our lives. He is always God even in our bad times. Jesus the same yesterday, today and forevermore. (Hebrews 13:8). He never changes. Because God, who is the object of our worship, is consistently who He is, our worship and praise must remain consistent. God is always good, and His intent is always good for us. His plan is always good and for our favor. His love is never-ending. These characteristics are a part of who God is. We must consume ourselves with pleasing Him with our praise and worship.

All of this was designed by the God of heaven and Earth to establish a pattern for worship forever. When we couple the Old Testament pattern with the New

Testament understanding, we are able to get a composite picture of what worship looks like when modeled after heaven.

Door 6

Face To Face

God knows everything about us, from the hairs on our heads, to the thoughts in our heads, before we can even think them. He knows every poor choice and mistake, and every desire spoken and unspoken. Why then do we hold back in our attempts to worship God? Relationship with God started in the garden with Adam and Eve both naked. Sin caused them to cover themselves. It was an attempt to hold something back from God.

Separation leads to hidden agendas and perspectives, but worshipping in spirit and truth allows our whole being to bow down before the King of Kings. All of our mistakes, faults, choices, and our positive and negative virtues are known by God. We must lay it down before Him and give Him all of us. God loves us perfectly in spite of our imperfections. That alone is enough for us to love, honor, worship and praise the Lord. Worshipers receive a reward for their pursuit of God. Hebrews 11:6 says, "You must first believe that He is (have confident faith in God's existence) and believe that God is a

48

rewarder of them that diligently seek Him". Psalms 16:11 "In His presence is fulness of joy and at His right hand are pleasures forever." Knowing that God's presence is our reward helps to settle why we pursue God daily. We must have joy in every situation, regardless of the prospective outlook. When the prize is presence, the pursuit becomes a desire and passion. David understood this and in Psalms 31 he says, "Early will I seek thee and daily I will worship." David purposed in his heart to seek God's presence, and he never allowed his situation to dictate the nature of his relationship with God. He committed to "bless The Lord at all times," and that God's praises "will continuously be in my mouth." (Psalms 34.) He continued, "Though a host should rise against me, in this will I be confident. One thing have I desired of The Lord and that will I seek after. That I may dwell in the house of The Lord all the days of my life to behold His beauty and to inquire in His temple." (Psalms 27). David declared even in the midst of war, his daily pursuit would be toward the face of God.

David's intent was to behold His beauty (Psalms 27:4). This deals with pursuit of the face of GOD not his hands. The face represents the visage, nature, and character of God. His face is not about His works. It's about the who of God not the what of God. In pursuit of God's face, we cannot settle for a shadow of God when He is available to be adored in person. The works of God are indicative of the One who has performed the work. We can't be so enamored with what He has done that we settle without actually encountering Him. If we can find God in worship and see His face while experiencing His presence, we will experience the works of His hands that are connected to His person. Settling for just the works of God will rob you of the benefit of relationship with Him. As our heavenly father, God wants to converse with us. He desires intimacy. The disciples understood that proximity to Jesus gave them an advantage in life. They learned how to operate like Jesus did. They reaped the rewards of proximity. They soon found themselves healing the sick and casting out demons. The more time they spent in the presence of the Lord, the more powerful they became. They shifted into greater.

We all have something in our lives that needs to be shifted and changed. God is the one who brings about that shift. Invite Him in and things will change. Worship has the ability to shift the trajectory of our lives propelling us into our destinies.

Isaiah had an encounter with God that transformed his thinking and opened his spirit to prophesy hundreds of

years into the future. The prophecy told of a coming
Messiah and literally defined, in detail, the assignment of
Jesus Christ. That encounter happened when King
Uzziah died. King Uzziah was a righteous leader who, in
a moment of pride, was stricken with leprosy. This
disease disqualified him from sitting on the throne. The
connection that Isaiah had with the king became a
distraction from a face-to-face encounter with God.

It wasn't until the king died that Isaiah realized that the
Lord was consistently present in the Tabernacle but
wasn't seen because life had altered the perception of
the prophet. The Lord was always high and lifted up.
The seraphim were always crying one to the other about
the holiness and glory of the Lord. The train of The Lord
had filled the temple. These things were present but the
prophet missed them because of distractions.

We often deal with major distractions that limit our ability
to see the face of the Lord. Worshippers must balance
what's present naturally and what must be discerned
spiritually or risk missing face to face encounters
designed to benefit them. Worship gives us access to the
presence of the Lord. The privilege of seeing Him high
and lifted up is more valuable than any other experience
in the church dynamic. We must get back to accessing

Access

the presence of the Lord and deliberately seeking His face.

Psalms 27:8 reminds us that the Lord desires for us to seek His face. We can't be so caught up in the blessings of His hands that we miss the grace of His face. Every person in the Bible who came in contact with the presence of Jesus in faith was changed indelibly. That same authority is available to us. The Syrophoenician woman who came to Jesus on behalf of her daughter worshipped and received a response in Mark 7. Her daughter was healed in that same hour. This woman knew that there was a blessing in seeking the face of Jesus. Though it wasn't her time, she knew a face to face encounter was the key to seeing real change in her family and, specifically, in her daughter.

Sometimes the greatest distraction is performance in our lives by the hand of the Lord. We can get stuck celebrating performance and miss the presence of the Lord. The wonders and works of God can be so overwhelming that we lose sight of His face when we view the spectacular power of His hands.

The Lord seeks opportunities to show Himself strong on our behalf. His eyes go throughout the whole Earth looking for a place to showcase His power. (2 Chronicles 16:9). He delights in working things out for His children. Our responsibility is the keep our eyes on Him and to give Him glory. We must continue to worship who He is as we praise what He does.

Even Moses had the privilege of face to face encounters. Exodus 33:11 tells us that God and Moses spoke to each other face to face as friends. Moses, at this point in his life, had seen multiple miraculous feats of the Lord. He did not, however, allow those miracles to reduce his relationship to performance of the power of the Lord. He continued to seek closer encounters by asking the Lord to show Moses His glory. (Exodus 33:18). Moses asked for something that would change the tenor of his relationship with The Lord. Jehovah responded by saying, "No man can see my face and live to tell it." The Lord told Moses that there was a place by Him in the mountain.

Maintaining face to face encounters with the Lord will often require us to leave our current level and ascend to higher planes. The Lord carved a place in the side of the mountain specifically to fit Moses. The Lord decided to allow His goodness to pass before Moses and allowed Moses see His back parts or His afterglow (Exodus

33:23). Moses was hidden in the cleft of the mountain and the Lord covered it with His hand until Moses could handle the encounter. This encounter was so significant for Moses that his face shined with the glory of God for an extended period of time. Face to face encounters leave lasting impressions on us. Moses didn't have to find proof that he and the Lord were meeting. The evidence was literally on his face. This same access has been given to us. We must be willing to ascend to the place where He is for a face to face meeting. Worship is the mechanism we use to go up.

Worship gives us unlimited access to His face. We must continue to pursue that place of privilege.

Door 7

Application

The Bible shows us that the Ark of the Testimony was designed to be carried by four Levites or Priests in the Old Testament. There are principles that we can find there that are really important in learning how to build a worship team and how to create synergy within that team. When we consider those that carry the Ark, there is something that we will never find in the bible. The four Levites that carried the Ark never stumbled. The Bible talks about it in 2 Samuel 6 and 1 Chronicles 13. King David went to retrieve the Ark of The Lord from Abinadab's house and put the Ark on a new cart. On the way to Jerusalem, the oxen stumbled at Nachon's threshing floor and the stumbling of the oxen caused Uzzah to put his hand on the Ark to steady it. "God smote Uzzah because of his offense," and He literally caused a breach to come upon one of His people. God does not need us to hold Him up or help Him stay balanced. He will never fall. God is creator of heaven and earth. Everything that we accomplish is by the word of His power. That is what He was saying when Uzzah touched the Ark.

He was saying, "Uzzah, I never need your hands to keep me up. That's not what you are there for. You're there to lift me up, but you don't keep me up!"

The Bible says that "David was afraid of God that day" because this was the first time in his life he had seen God angry. He had never understood the anger of God. He'd seen the benefit of God, the love of God, the restorative power of God, the covering God, and the victory of God. But he had never seen God angry. The reason he'd never seen God angry is because he had never chosen to do something that was diametrically opposed to God's decree with regard to worship and with regard to the transporting of the Ark.

The Ark remained at Obededom's house for 90 days, and God blessed Obededom's house, and everything that pertained to Obededom's house was blessed because of the Ark of the Covenant being there. After hearing about what went on in the place where the Ark rested, of course David went back to retrieve the Ark and have it rest in the City of David. The Bible says David did his research and did something very significant. He told everybody to sanctify themselves. David instructed all of the Levites that sanctification and holy living was requisite to qualify to transport the glory of the Lord represented in the Ark. He told them that they were not going to try to transport the Ark on a cart; Instead, they would utilize the poles or the staves that were in the Ark and four men would carry it. The principle was this:

1. The Ark was never supposed to be pulled behind beasts who have no idea or concept of the magnitude of who God is

2. Animals also have no regard for where they relieve themselves.

Anyone who has ever been on a horse-drawn carriage knows that the horses just defecate wherever they want. The presence of God should never be around foul-smelling waste of any kind! That is especially offensive. If it is offensive to us, imagine just how offensive it is to God. There is a definitive line that has to be drawn as worship leaders. We can't operate like beasts, where we utilize no discretion regarding our walk, nor can we operate from the perspective that we don't have a concept of who God is. We also cannot operate from the perspective that God does not deserve a greater place of esteem.

God says if you are ever going to transport My glory,

what you have to do is lift me up above men. Four men must carry the Ark on their shoulders. This means that the heads of the men are never higher than the Ark. The principle is no human, human mechanism, human thought, or human concept is greater than the grace, the glory, and the power of God.

This is vital to the narrative. The oxen stumbled (1 Chronicles 13:9). So when we operate callously, the potential for stumbling is always present. It is never recorded in the Bible that those who carried the Ark of the Covenant ever stumbled. It never happened! If four men carried the glory of God, understanding the weight and responsibility, the weight alone challenges the carrier to be circumspect. When someone gets under the weight of the glory of God, it automatically institutes the desire to be meticulous in operation in their heart, their mind, and their spirit. Many times, when we desire the presence of the Lord during worship, we do things with little or no regard for the Lord. We sing songs that fit an old paradigm which means we are not being careful what God is doing in the present. If we are not careful, we will begin to operate like beasts, and eventually we will stumble if we continue in that regard. The key for us to understand is that it's a privilege to bear the weight of the glory of God, and the privilege is a responsibility. If we fail to operate as if the privilege is a responsibility, we risk taking it for granted. We are going to become common and far too familiar with it. We are going to do things under the glory that are counterintuitive to who God is and HE is going to start smelling our stuff!

We can't have people on our teams who are not willing to bear the responsibility of carrying the weight. If you are not willing to bear the responsibility of carrying the weight, then, perhaps, you aren't ready to participate on the team. This is not just the person leading the song, this is the whole team. We often think if someone is leading a song of worship, they're the only one in front. No. Everybody is up front. Everyone is being equally scrutinized.

This includes:

Musicians
Praise and worship leader and team
Dancers
Flag bearers
Mimes
No matter what someone is doing or what vernacular is used, it's the team. Everyone involved in praise and worship should be prepared and willing to carry the Ark.

As worshippers, we have to be willing to pay attention to the other people who are also carrying of the Ark because it takes a team to perform this task. Everybody who is on the team has to pay attention to their peers. This involves the responsibility of accountability, a concept perceived like a curse word in the church. We don't like accountability, but it is what ensures sobriety and humility. If any one person can do whatever they want to do and nobody checks them, everybody is wrong! The whole is intrinsically impacted negatively by the sum of its parts.

Here is the key: If someone knows another is doing wrong, but they don't pull the offender on the carpet, the whole team is going to be relegated to the same low level that the offender is on. A chain is only as strong as its weakest link. We've got to see this. If we aren't willing to hold each other accountable, we're literally saying we agree with whatever the offender is doing. The pastor shouldn't have to come and sit people down for the sake of a look or a feel when the praise team itself should hold each other accountable.

Here is what's going to happen. If someone gets weak holding up their end of the Ark, the Ark is going to tilt. It is not ideal for anyone leading worship with a tilted Ark.

Access

Everyone has to do their part and accept collective responsibility. If we hold each other accountable and we are praying together—doing all the things necessary to maintain a high level of personal integrity regarding worship—the whole house will receive the benefit of the Ark being appropriately carried.

Here's what happens when the team works together according to Joshua 3: God told Joshua, "Tell the people when they see the Ark moving, they are to leave their place and go after the Ark. Tell them not to get too close because I am taking them a way that they have never been before." This is absolutely imperative for all of us. The people see the Ark moving, and it is moving because the Levites are carrying it. Here is the privilege of being a glory carrier: We get to witness, firsthand, the move of God— the miracles and the ability of God to be made manifest.

The Bible says that when the soles of the feet of the priests who were carrying the Ark hit the edge of the river Jordan, the whole river responded by backing up over a mile away to a city called Ad'am. Israel witnessed a river moving in the wrong direction because the carriers of the Ark were operating in concert and accountability. Because they did not act as beasts, they did not stumble as they led the nation of Israel to a new place.

It's important for us to understand that when we, as glory carriers, operate in concert, exercise accountability, and behave as like-minded men with an understanding, we can release miracles. The whole house can be shifted. If we want our churches to shift, we need to check and see if there are any "beasts" on the praise team. Beasts are people who have such a low, uneducated, unfiltered understanding of who God is, that they don't recognize His power and they don't recognize His value. They don't recognize the fact that God should be honored or that their lack of knowledge stinks to people and, much worse, to God.

It is important for us to understand that if we are going to be the kind of worship leaders that we are supposed to be in this modern day era, we must go back to concepts like sanctification, consecration, prayer, accountability, love, and honesty. We must be honest enough to say, "Hey I'm not right, and I might stumble if I try to carry the Ark today. I'm going to take off today." It takes a lot of courage and integrity to say, "You know what, today is not my day."

Singing a song is not about being skillful in using

melismatic, rhythmic, lyrical lines. It's about being able to introduce and present the glory of God in a cogent, salient, tangible way every time we stand before His people. When we do that, it changes the dynamic of our worship experience. As a glory carrier, we are under one of the corners of the Ark. We are a pillar for worship, for praise, and for accountability. We have to be intelligent and prudent enough to make good decisions about how we engage in worship. In a corporate group of worship leaders, who the team is comprised of matters. It's not just about who has the best voices; It's about people who know how to be accountable and how to handle the weight of the glory. Someone may not have the best voice, but if they have a heart after God, that's where the grace comes in. The grace will cover bad notes and limitations. It will cause everybody to step into a place of a new move, a fresh move of God.

The link between the pastor and minister of music or lead musician must be cohesive because that relationship in the church can have lasting effects on the solidarity of the worship experience. In 1 Chronicles 15, King David appointed Chenaniah as his chief Levite who would take charge of those who transported the Ark and the music that accompanied that movement. Chenaniah was for song, and his ears were tuned into the sound of heaven.

He was skilled in the song of the Lord and was astute enough to train and teach others how to release the sound of heaven on Earth.

This is vitally important today. We must be keen in hearing and releasing the sound of heaven. We must hear the songs that please the Lord and repeat them. Too often, we sing songs that entice the flesh or comes from what is a Top 30 radio hit. Though the songs we often hear are good songs, they don't always indicate that the anointing of God rests at their release. We must be extremely careful not to do what's popular at the cost of the anointing.

The relationship between pastor and minister of music must contain several core elements to ensure maximum effectiveness. First, there must be a connection. This connection is more than a cursory handshake and hello, and it should foster trust and implicit adherence to the leadership of the pastor. The pastor must also be open to the suggestions that may be on the heart of the minister of music. Chenaniah was trusted with transporting the glory of the Lord represented by the Ark of the Covenant. This freed the hands of the King to lead the whole nation and avoid focusing on just the music department or sacred arts. David was skilled as a musician and songwriter, however, he was confident in the connection that he had with Chenaniah.

Confidence is the second attribute that must be present in the relationship between the pastor and minister of music. Confidence allowed Chenaniah to complete his assignment without David micromanaging the entire effort. It gave David the ability to look at all the aspects of carrying the Ark from Obed-Edom's home to the City of David where the resting place for the Ark was in the hill of The Lord. David was able to lead the people in worship and dancing while Chenaniah led the Levites in movement and song. Confidence is fostered by the third component.

Third, there must be communication. It is clear that David and Chenaniah conversed regularly. Chenaniah was trained and skilled, but David had to know the heart of the person who would lead the Levites. The last time David tried to transport the Ark, he and the people suffered the loss of Uzzah, who put his hand on the Ark at the threshing floor. For the offense, the Lord made a breach on Uzzah and killed him at the threshing floor. The Lord had instructed that no one should casually put their hands on the Ark. Uzzah broke that rule. There's a lesson here: Familiarity with the glory of the Lord can lead to heartbreaking results. This principle also translates to the worship leader and pastor. This isn't an indicator that we can't be friends with the leaders, however, it speaks to the need to understand roles and responsibilities. Friendship can't blur the lines of authority when leadership makes a decision that those who follow may not like. Breaches are avoidable when communication is at the forefront of the relationship between pastor and minister of music or chief worship leader.

Being able to manage this connection will foster growth in the things of the Lord and a healthy regard for and sensitivity to the presence of the Lord. The song of the Lord will flow freely and the blessing and anointing that breaks yokes will be present both inside and outside the church walls.

Conclusion

These 7 doors are designed to bring enlightenment and hope to all who participate in worship and praise. My hope is that every reader develops a new level of confidence in their individual and corporate pursuits of the presence of the Lord. I pray that the context of worship becomes so enhanced that the world receives the benefit of the clarity that I believe this book will bring.

Pray this prayer with me:

Lord Jesus, thank You for gifting me with the ability to release a sound on Earth. Thank you for choosing to use me as a conduit for worship and praise. Help me to submit fully to Your will for my life. Open my eyes to any area that requires change, repentance, or a new way of thinking. Forgive me for all of the times that pride became a way of life for me. Forgive me for every time I placed something in my life more important than You. Anoint me afresh and allow Your power to flow through me in a supernatural way. Flow through me. Use me for Your glory.
Amen.

About The Author

Jason Nelson is the pastor of The Tabernacle, a thriving ministry in Windsor Mill, Maryland near Baltimore. He has served in this capacity for more than a decade while also being a global figure in the music industry. His love for worship developed in church at an early age where he began as a singer and musician. Eventually, he would become the minister of music developing the ability to compose and lead others. Today, Jason is a sought after voice in the Gospel community. An acclaimed singer and song writer, Jason has received a Stellar Award in addition to being both a Grammy Award nominated songwriter and Dove Award Nominee. His award winning worship has birthed several songs and albums which have landed at #1 on Billboard charts. Jason's career spans decades and throughout the journey, he has amassed knowledge that benefits the global community of musicians and worship leaders. He has been married to his wife, Tonya Nelson, for 23 years. Together, they have 2 children, Jaelyn Paris and Jason Christopher.

Website: www.JnelsonOnline.com
Instagram: PastorJNelson
Twitter: PastorJNelson
Facebook: Jason Nelson Music